DATE DUE

			PRINTED IN U.S.A.

Chris Paul

SUPERSTARS IN THE WORLD OF BASKETBALL

SUPERSTARS IN THE WORLD OF BASKETBALL

Chris Paul

Aurelia Jackson

Mason Crest

Mason Crest
450 Parkway Drive, Suite D
Broomall, PA 19008
www.masoncrest.com

Printed and bound in the United States of America.

First printing
9 8 7 6 5 4 3 2 1

Series ISBN: 978-1-4222-3101-2
ISBN: 978-1-4222-3104-3
ebook ISBN: 978-1-4222-8794-1

The Library of Congress has cataloged the
hardcopy format(s) as follows:
        Library of Congress Cataloging-in-Publication Data

Jackson, Aurelia.
   Chris Paul / Aurelia Jackson.
      pages cm. — (Superstars in the world of basketball)
   ISBN 978-1-4222-3104-3 (hardback) — ISBN 978-1-4222-3101-2 (series) 1. Paul, Chris, 1985–Juvenile literature. 2. Basketball players—United States—Biography—Juvenile literature. I. Title.
   GV884.P376J34 2015
   796.323092—dc23
   [B]
                                                  2014005513

Contents

KEY ICONS TO LOOK FOR:

Text-Dependent Questions: These questions send the reader back to the text for more careful attention to the evidence presented there.

Words to Understand: These words with their easy-to-understand definitions will increase the reader's understanding of the text, while building vocabulary skills.

Series Glossary of Key Terms: This back-of-the book glossary contains terminology used throughout this series. Words found here increase the reader's ability to read and comprehend higher-level books and articles in this field.

Research Projects: Readers are pointed toward areas of further inquiry connected to each chapter. Suggestions are provided for projects that encourage deeper research and analysis.

Sidebars: This boxed material within the main text allows readers to build knowledge, gain insights, explore possibilities, and broaden their perspectives by weaving together additional information to provide realistic and holistic perspectives.

Words to Understand

commissioner: A person in charge of regulating a particular sport.

idols: People you admire and want to imitate.

varsity: A first-string sports team that represents a high school or college.

Big Dreams

Chris Paul takes a deep breath and looks up to the stands. All eyes are on him. He is standing in the middle of a large Houston arena at the end of the 2013 NBA All-Star weekend. As an NBA All-Star, Chris is used to the attention.

NBA ALL-STAR MVP

The NBA All-Star Games take place once a year. The best players in the NBA are voted onto the NBA All-Star teams by their fans. The players are divided into the Eastern and Western division based on the team they play for in the NBA. Chris is on the NBA All-Star West team, because he plays for the Los Angeles Clippers.

Chris waits patiently for the NBA All-Star Game's most valuable player (MVP) to be announced. This is the player who did the most to help his team win. This can be through scoring points, assisting others, stealing the ball from opponents, or blocking shots. Standing

DATE February

PAY TO THE ORDER OF Boys & Girls Clubs of America & NO KID HUNGRY $ 35

Three Hundred Fifty Thousand Dollars and OO/100

FOR BOYS & GIRLS CLUBS OF AMERICA

Chris holds the 2013 NBA All-Star Game trophy while he presents a check to the Boys and Girls Clubs of America from State Farm Insurance.

Make Connections

In a basketball game, ten people play on the court at a time. They are split up into two teams of five players. Teammates must work together to score baskets. They all have different roles to play. One teammate may pass the ball to another teammate before a shot is made. The passer will do this if his teammate has an open shot to score. If the person who catches the ball shoots and scores a point, the person who passed him the ball is awarded an assist. Players who perform assists are very important. They help set the shooter up for a perfect shot. Chris Paul is one of the best assisters in the NBA.

next to Chris is David Stern, the NBA *commissioner*. Behind him are members from the West team. The West beat the East by five points.

Chris was a big part of why the West won the game. The team's other starters were Kobe Bryant, Kevin Durant, Blake Griffin, and Dwight Howard. A starter is someone who plays at the beginning of a game. He usually plays during any other important moments, such as the very end when every point counts. He usually has the best personal record out of every person on the team.

Everything gets quiet as David Stern begins to speak. "With 20 points, 15 assists, 4 steals, Chris Paul is the most valuable player of the 2013 NBA All-Star Game." Commissioner Stern hands Chris a large trophy, while his fans cheer. He holds the glass trophy above his head and smiles. Even with the award in his hands, he still can't believe it. "This is crazy," he says in an interview. "You never expect something like this."

Chris has played in a total of six All-Star games as of 2013, but this was his first time being named the most valuable player. He only scored a total of 20 points in the game, but that isn't what makes him special. Chris is best known for his assists. His career average is almost 10 assists per game. The only two people to ever achieve a higher assist average are Magic Johnson and John Stockton. Both are now retired. This means that Chris holds the record for the highest assists per game of any active NBA player.

At the age of just twenty-eight, Chris had come very far in his career. He always dreamed of joining the NBA, but there were times when he wasn't sure if he would make it. He was always very small compared to his peers. He is only six feet tall. Though this may be tall compared to an average human, it's not for professional basketball players! Chris is actually very short compared to other NBA players. NBA players tend to be tall. The extra height gives them an advantage over opponents. They can shoot over another player's head or reach up to block an opponent's shot.

Because Chris is shorter than most players, he has to work extra hard. Chris is a point

Chris has worked hard to become the successful player fans love today. As a young person, Chris practiced hard to be the best player he could, making sure he had the best chance to make it to the NBA.

guard. Point guards help their teammates score by bringing the ball down the court and passing it to someone who is in a perfect position to shoot and score. Sometimes, point guards take shots, too. Point guards need to be fast on their feet and able to think quickly. They are often team leaders, because they need to make decisions for their teammates. And Chris is considered one of the best in the NBA.

Chris first discovered basketball as a child. He decided then and there that he was going to join the NBA one day. Chris knew it wouldn't be easy. Becoming a professional athlete is a lot of hard work. Chris began training early with the help of his father, who happened to be a coach and former athlete. He practiced for hours every day to make himself a better player. Chris was just twenty years old when he joined the NBA draft in 2005. Since then, he has earned multiple NBA and world titles, including two Olympic gold medals.

A YOUNG ATHLETE

Christopher Emmanuel Paul was born on May 6, 1985, in Lewisville, North Carolina. His parents, Charles and Robin, were childhood friends before they fell in love and got married. Chris has an older brother named Charles, but everyone calls him C.J., because he has the same name as his father. C.J. is two years older than Chris.

Chris's father was an athlete long before he settled down and had children. His two favorite sports were basketball and football. Growing up, Chris and C.J. learned a lot about sports from their father. Charles was even their coach when they were young.

Chris first picked up basketball when he was just three years old. One day, his father bought a pair of plastic baskets and set up a basketball court in the family's basement. Charles used tape to draw the lines for the court and encouraged his sons to play. Chris and C.J. spent hours in the basement, practicing how to shoot.

It wasn't long before Chris and C.J. both dreamed of playing basketball on a real team. They watched NBA games on television together. Two of Chris's favorite players

Magic Johnson is one of the most famous basketball players of all time. His amazing skills on the court have inspired millions of young players over the years.

Text-Dependent Questions

1. What is the NBA All-Star Game? How are players chosen for it?
2. What is an MVP? Who was named MVP in the 2013 NBA All-Star Game?
3. When Chris was young, what kept him from being as good at basketball as other sports?
4. What did Chris's grandfather do for a living? What did Chris learn from working for his grandfather?
5. Why couldn't Chris join the varsity basketball team during his freshman year of high school?

were Michael Jordan and Magic Johnson. He looked up to them and hoped to be just as great one day. Chris was already great at shooting baskets, but he had just one problem. He wasn't big like his basketball *idols*. Professional basketball players are tall and muscular. Chris was small and short. If Chris wanted to join the NBA, he needed to grow up to be big and strong.

Chris's size did not stop him from doing well in other sports. He was fast on his feet and good at catching, which made him great at playing football. He joined a peewee team, the Lewisville Titans, when he was a young boy. Chris had a lot of energy on the field and rarely needed to take a break during a game. He played quarterback, linebacker, and running back. These positions are usually played by someone who is great at catching the football and running fast. The Lewisville Titans did so well while Chris was a part of the team that they made it to a national championship.

Charles did his best to support his sons when they played. He went to any game he could. Charles and Robin also taught their sons good manners and the importance of getting an education. They created very strict rules for their sons to follow. Video games were only allowed on the weekend. Chris and C.J. had to study hard and get good grades. If they started slacking off, their parents punished them.

HARD WORK

The Paul family believed in spending a lot of time with each other. One of the most important people in Chris's life was his grandfather. His name was Nathaniel, and he was Robin's father. Nathaniel Jones lived in Winston-Salem, where Charles and Robin grew up. He owned Jones Chevron, a service station for cars. Customers came to the shop to buy gasoline and change the oil in their cars.

Chris's dreams of playing basketball in the NBA seemed far away for the five-foot-one high school freshman.

Nathaniel's shop was very popular, and so was he. Nathaniel was the first African American in North Carolina to own a service station of his own. Plenty of people looked up to him for owning a business and for being so kind. Nathaniel treated his customers well. When times were tough, Nathaniel would let customers take gasoline without asking for anything in return. He even gave people money right out of the cash register if they needed it.

Nathaniel was known by the community as Papa Chili. Chris saw Papa Chili as his role model. The two were very close while Chris was growing up. Chris and C.J. chatted with their grandfather while helping out at the shop. Some of their duties included changing oil and rotating tires. This taught Chris that hard work can be rewarding, a lesson he would use to help him make it to the NBA. He also learned that it's important to share the money you earn with others.

As Chris grew older, he became more and more afraid of not being able to play basketball because of his height. His family encouraged Chris to keep trying. When Chris entered high school, he was only five-foot-one. This is well below average for even a high school basketball player. Chris wasn't picked for the *varsity* team. Instead, he joined the junior varsity team. Chris would have to wait for his time to shine.

BEATING THE ODDS

Chris entered West Forsyth High School in 1999. He was already a very skilled basketball player, but he just didn't have the height to make it onto the varsity team. Varsity teams only take the best players in the entire high school. Athletes who want to join the varsity team need to try out before they can join. Chris's brother, C.J., was the star of the varsity team, which included players up to the age of eighteen.

HIGH SCHOOL BASKETBALL

Athletes who aren't skilled or big enough to join the varsity team have the option of joining a junior varsity team. Junior varsity teams help athletes train to be better so they can earn a spot onto a varsity team. Junior varsity teams play games against junior varsity teams from other schools. Chris joined the junior varsity team in his freshman year and played on it for two years. He saw this as a chance to gain experience and get better at playing with other high school students on the court.

After his growth spurt, Chris's dream of playing basketball in high school was closer than ever.

Chris grew almost ten inches by the end of his sophomore year. With his skills—and now his growth spurt—it was more than enough to make it onto the varsity team. Unfortunately, he didn't get to play with his older brother very often on a real team. C.J. graduated at the end of Chris's sophomore year. Chris began playing with the varsity team at the start of his junior year. When C.J. left, it gave Chris Paul a chance to show his school what he was made of.

Chris had a very good first season. He averaged a total of 25 points, 5 assists, and over 4 steals per game. The West Forsyth team also had a great year. They had 26 wins and only 4 losses. Chris and his teammates did so well that they made it to the state semifinals. By this point, Chris and his family knew he had a real shot at joining the NBA.

The summer before Chris's senior year was a busy one. He was selected as the MVP of the U-17 National Championship in 2002 while playing for the Kappa Magic team. He continued practicing and getting better at his favorite sport while looking into colleges to attend at the same time. Wake Forest University was his top choice, because it had a great basketball team and was close to where he grew up. During that summer, he signed a letter agreeing to play for the team after high school.

POINTS FOR PAPA CHILI

Attending Wake Forest University was a very big decision for Chris. His family was very proud of how far he had come and couldn't wait to see what he did on a college team. Unfortunately, there was no time to celebrate. One of the most important people in Chris's life died the day after Chris signed the papers. Papa Chili was murdered during a violent robbery by a gang of teenagers. He was only sixty-one years old. The community lost a great man. Almost two thousand people went to Nathanial Jones' funeral a few days later.

The entire Paul family was broken up by Nathaniel Jones' death. Nathaniel was more than a grandfather to Chris. He was an inspiration. Papa Chili always encouraged Chris to do his best on the court and in all other areas of his life. When Chris was scared he wouldn't be tall enough to join the NBA, Papa Chili told him to keep trying. Now that man was gone.

The Paul family needed time to heal, but Chris did not have that kind of time. The new basketball season was starting very soon. Chris was entering his senior year and wanted to play in every game he could. He knew if Papa Chili were alive, he would tell Chris to keep following his dream. So Chris wanted to find a way to honor his grandfather on the court. He and his aunt came up with a great idea. Chris would score one point for every year his grandfather was alive in just one game.

Papa Chili was sixty-one when he died. Scoring 61 points in one game seemed almost impossible to Chris. He averaged only 25 points per game in his junior year. He would have to score more than double that amount to reach his goal. But Chris surprised

Going to Wake Forest University was a big change for Chris. But playing basketball at Wake Forest was another step toward Chris's dream of playing in the NBA.

During sports, fouls sometimes happen. Fouls are anything that is not allowed during a game. Sometimes, fouls are accidental. At other times, they are on purpose. Tripping or pushing another teammate is considered a foul. Players who commit a foul are punished. Usually, they have to sit out for a certain amount of time from that game, but if the foul is really bad, the player may be suspended from other games, too.

everyone during the first game of the season, when he hit his mark. He scored 32 points in the first half! Once he reached 61 points in the second half, he left the game in tears. He had done what he set out to do. Papa Chili would have been proud. This proved to Chris that he could do anything he set his mind to. He just needed to want it enough. Chris became even more determined to join the NBA after that game.

As extraordinary as Chris was in the first game of the season, the year was far from over. His average points per game jumped up to 30 that year. He also scored more that 8 assists and 5 rebounds per game. Chris was named to the *USA Today*'s All-USA high school second team. He became North Carolina's Mr. Basketball and High School Player of the Year.

Before Chris went to college, he played on the East team in the 2003 McDonald's High School All-American Game. One of the people he played with that year was LeBron James. Like Chris, LeBron went on to become a famous basketball player. Chris scored 10 assists in the game. He didn't care about scoring as much as he cared about setting up his teammates for the perfect shot. This earned him the game's sportsmanship award. With so many awards under his belt, Chris was more than ready to play for a college team.

WAKE FOREST UNIVERSITY

One of the reasons Chris chose Wake Forest University is because of its location close to home. Another reason was Wake Forest University's coach. Chris wanted to train under Skip Prosser, the head coach of the Demon Deacons basketball team. The two first met while Chris was in high school. By the time Chris actually started playing for the Demon Deacons, he was well known by his future teammates. The Deacons were excited to play with him.

Chris began as a point guard at Wake Forest University. It was the perfect position for him. He would get to pass a lot and dash down the court. His height was not an issue,

Famous Wake Forest basketball coach Skip Prosser pushed Chris to be the best player he could be. Skip died in 2007, just a short time after he coached Chris at Wake Forest.

Research Project

After Chris helped the Wake Forest University team be successful, they retired his jersey, meaning that no future players on the team could have his number. Go online and see if any jerseys have been retired for NBA teams. What are some of the reasons that a jersey might be retired?

because he didn't shoot as much as his other teammates. He also wasn't expected to block opponents from shooting. Chris worked well with fellow teammate Justin Gray, who was great at shooting. Together, they could line up almost any shot. At six feet tall, Chris earned his fair share of points.

The Demon Deacons did well the year Chris joined the team, and the world noticed. Chris averaged almost 15 points and 6 assists per game, making him one of the best college rookies in the country. Rookies are first-year players, usually freshmen. Chris was named the Atlantic Coast Conference (ACC) Rookie of the Year. He also became the National Freshman of the Year. He broke many Wake Forest University freshman records. Chris logged more free throws, assists, and steals than any freshman in Wake Forest history.

Some basketball players play on a university team for just one year. Others stay for the full four or five years. This gives NBA scouts time to notice college players. Athletes also use this time to practice and gain more experience. But if the athlete is talented enough, he may choose to leave the university before he is ready to graduate. Chris was doing well at Wake Forest University, and he decided to stay for a second year.

Chris did not get off to a great start in his sophomore year. During a heated game, he punched an opponent in the stomach. This is an illegal move, known as a foul, and a very serious one. Chris was suspended from the game for fouling another player. Before this happened, Chris was a well-liked player and a great leader. He led his teammates to many victories. Chris would need to make up for what he did if he was going to fix his public image. He apologized for his actions and tried to move on. Fortunately for Chris, his fans forgave him.

Chris received a lot of attention during his 2004–2005 season. That's why he decided to join the NBA draft at the end of the sophomore year. He felt he had done everything he could in college and was ready to move on to a *professional* league. NBA scouts agreed. Plenty of cities wanted to bring Chris to their team, including the New Orleans

Playing basketball for Wake Forest helped Chris become the player fans know today. Chris works to send students to Wake Forest University through his scholarship program, so that other young people can have the same education Chris had.

Text-Dependent Questions

1. What is a junior varsity team?
2. Why did Chris have a goal of scoring 61 points in one game?
3. Why did Chris decide to go to Wake Forest University?
4. Why did Chris have trouble during the beginning of his sophomore year?
5. What reasons did Chris have for joining the NBA draft at the end of his sophomore year in college?

Hornets, Atlanta Hawks, and Charlotte Bobcats. Chris finished his second and final year at Wake Forest University and joined the NBA draft in 2005. In 2013 Wake Forest University retired Chris's jersey number as a way to honor him.

His years playing for Wake Forest University were successful. But it was now time to fulfill a lifelong dream.

 Words to Understand

roster: A list or plan that shows the order in which players will take their turn.

NBA Career

The NBA draft is held every year in June. Chris joined the draft in 2005. Each team takes turns picking new members during the draft rounds. The teams with the worst record get to pick first. Chris was so successful during college that a lot of teams couldn't wait to bring him onto the team. He was chosen fourth out of all the players who entered the draft that year. The New Orleans Hornets was anxious to add him to its *roster*.

The Hornets play in Louisiana, a state in the southern region of the United States. Chris would miss his family, but he always knew this day would come. Professional basketball players who join the draft must move wherever their team takes them. Chris was excited to start his new life as a professional basketball player. He packed his bags and prepared to move to New Orleans. No one could have predicted what would happen next.

In August of 2005, Hurricane Katrina struck the southern United States. It was one of the deadliest hurricanes in the United States ever. Though New Orleans avoided serious damage from Katrina, levees protecting the city failed, flooding parts of the city and

Chris's time with Hornets was a mix of highs and lows. Chris played well, but the team didn't always do as well as he would have liked.

killing many people. Some parts of New Orleans were completely destroyed.

It would take years to rebuild New Orleans, but the Hornets needed to play now more than ever. The people of the city needed something to look forward to. The Hornets couldn't play on their usual court, so they found another place to practice. Oklahoma City became the team's temporary home. The Hornets worked hard to make the city of New Orleans proud, but none more than Chris.

Chris had a great first year with the Hornets, even if he didn't get to play in Louisiana most of the time. He averaged 16 points, almost 8 assists, and 5 rebounds by the end of the season. His performance during the 2005–2006 season earned him the NBA's 2006 Rookie of the Year Award. He was also named the Rookie of the Month during every single month that year. Chris even scored his first triple-double in his rookie year.

NEW ORLEANS HORNETS

Chris did so well in his first season that his fans knew he could only get better. His average points and assists per game increased during his second season. Unfortunately, he didn't get to play much. Playing sports comes with certain risks. Players can injure themselves at any time. When an athlete is injured, he cannot play until his injury heals. Chris hurt himself a few times during the 2006–2007 season. He was forced to sit out for almost twenty games that year.

The Hornets did not do very well without Chris' help. The team did not make it to the playoffs, winning only thirty-nine games that year. This was just one more game than the last season. Chris and the rest of the Hornets were determined to change that in the 2007–2008 season, and they did not disappoint their fans. The season began with the Hornets moving back to New Orleans. The New Orleans arena was finally repaired and ready to use. The Hornets were able to practice and play in their home city once again.

The year started off well. Chris increased his average to 21 points per game. He had the highest average assists of anyone in the NBA that year, with almost 12 per game. His steals were also the highest in the NBA, at just under 3. This earned him a spot on the

Chris dribbles during a game against Spain in the 2008 Summer Olympic Games in Beijing, China.

West team in the 2008 NBA All-Star Game, which happened to take place in New Orleans that year. The West team did not win, but it did come close. The East won 134–128.

The Hornets won fifty-six games in Chris's third year. He became known as a leader who wasn't shy about passing the ball to his teammates. He didn't care who on his team scored—as long as the point was made, and the Hornets won the game. The Hornets made it to the playoffs that year. The team beat the Dallas Mavericks in the first few games but eventually lost to the San Antonio Spurs.

Chris was not upset when the Hornets lost the playoffs. The team had gotten much better since Chris joined three years before, and he hoped it would continue to improve. The Hornets would have another chance at the NBA championship next year. That's why Chris decided to re-sign with the Hornets. He was proud to be part of the team and wanted to see how far he could get with his teammates. Chris signed on for three more years. His new contract earned him a total of almost $70 million. That's over $23 million a year!

Every basketball player has different strengths and weaknesses. Some players are better at scoring, while others are better at passing and stealing. Chris showed his strengths in the 2007–2008 season and continued to improve them the next season. He led the NBA with the highest average assists and steals for a second year in a row, during the 2008–2009 season. Chris even made history when he became the first person in the NBA to score 27 points, 10 rebounds, and 15 assists in a single game. He scored more triple-doubles that year, which showed that he was a very versatile player. Versatile players are good at all areas of a sport.

Chris kept getting better and hoped the Hornets would do the same. Unfortunately, the Hornets did not do much better than the year before. The Hornets won forty-nine games in the regular season, which was enough to make it to the NBA playoffs. The team was quickly eliminated, though, in the first set of games against the Denver Nuggets.

By the end of the 2008–2009 season, it was clear that Chris was best at playing defense. He was selected to the NBA All-Defensive first team and All-NBA second team. Defensive players steal the ball from opponents, block shots, pass the ball to teammates, and bring the basketball back down the court.

The 2009–2010 season did not start off well. The Hornet's head coach, Byron Scott, was blamed for the losses. He was fired after the first few games of the season. Jeff Bower replaced him, and Chris Paul was not happy about it. He thought Scott was doing a fine job. After all, the team had improved quite a lot while Byron was the head coach.

Chris didn't play very well in the 2009–2010 season, mostly because he wasn't able to. He was injured twice that year and missed more games than any other season. First, he sprained his ankle, which forced him to sit out eight games. Later, he injured his knee. The injury was so serious that Chris needed surgery to fix it. He had the operation in February of 2010 and was stuck on the bench for almost two months.

Chris was named an NBA All-Star for a third time since 2008. But injuries kept him out of the game. Chauncey Billups replaced him.

After leaving the New Orleans Hornets, Chris moved to Los Angeles to play for the L.A. Clippers.

The Hornets did not do very well without Chris and only won thirty-seven games that year. They all looked forward to the next season. Chris and his teammates saw the 2010–2011 season as a chance for the Hornets to bounce back. The team won forty-six games that year and easily made it to the playoffs. The first team they faced happened to be the defending champion of the last two years. The Hornets hard to beat the Los Angeles Lakers but were unable to win. Chris averaged 22 points and almost 12 assists in the playoffs.

LOS ANGELES CLIPPERS

By the start of the 2011–2012 season, Chris was ready for a change. He had played for the New Orleans Hornets since 2005, the year he entered the NBA. The team had gotten better over the years but not enough to keep up with Chris. The Hornets were afraid they would lose Chris after his contract was up. Management decided to trade him to another team before that happened, so Chris was traded to the Los Angeles Clippers. Hornets fans were unhappy about Chris leaving. He was one of the best players the team had, and he had done a lot to help rebuild the city after Hurricane Katrina.

Chris was happy about joining the Clippers. It was the change of pace he hoped would help him win his first NBA championship. Chauncey Billups and Blake Griffin joined Chris as new members of the Clippers. Chris chose to finish out his original New Orleans contract, which would keep him with the Clippers for at least two years. In the 2012–2013 season, the Clippers made it to the Western Conference playoffs but lost against the Memphis Grizzlies.

Chris became a free agent in 2013, when his contract ended. His fans were not sure if Chris would re-sign with the Clippers. After all, the team had not come any closer to winning a championship than the Hornets had. His fans were relieved and happy when Chris announced in July of 2013 that he would be signing a five-year contract with the Clippers, worth over $100 million.

In 2012, Chris played for Team USA in the Olympics again, playing with superstars like LeBron James and Carmelo Anthony.

INTERNATIONAL GAMES

Chris is no stranger to international championships. He began competing for the United States before he was even twenty years old. His first international competition was in 2004, when his team won the FIBA Americas U20 Championship. At nineteen years old, he brought home his first gold medal. Two years later, he earned a bronze medal in the FIBA World Championship in Japan. That time, he competed with players of all ages.

Chris has competed for the United States in two Olympic Games. The first was in 2008, and the second was in 2012. The US basketball team took home a gold medal both times. In 2008 Chris averaged more assists than any other member of the US team.

Words to Understand

passions: The things you're excited about.
motivation: Reason for doing something.

CHRIS PAUL TODAY

Chris met his wife in 2003, while they were both students at Wake Forest University. Her name is Jada Cawley. One of the reasons Chris loves Jada is because she was with him before he became a star. He has said, "Jada was with me when I was broke." She stood by him as he struggled to make it into the NBA. Chris and Jada had their first child in 2009, while Chris was still playing for the Hornets. Their first son is named Christopher Emmanuel Paul II, after his father.

STARTING A FAMILY

Chris married Jada in September of 2011. The wedding was held in North Carolina so that family and friends could attend. The couple had a second child, Camryn Alexis Paul, in 2012. By this point, they had moved to Los Angeles. Chris bought a mansion for the family in Bel Air, one of the most expensive neighborhoods in Los Angeles. The house cost over $8 million.

In 2005, Hurricane Katrina cost many people in New Orleans everything, destroying their homes and tossing their lives into chaos. The stories of survivors pushed Chris to do all he could to help the people of New Orleans after Katrina.

Many basketball players have a nickname. Chris's nickname on the court is CP3. The nickname comes from his name, Chris Paul, and his jersey number, 3. Whenever Chris would score a basket while playing for the Hornets, the announcer would simply say, "CP3," and the crowd would cheer.

Family has always been the most important thing in Chris Paul's life. Chris knows he wouldn't have made it into the NBA without his family's help. In a 2007 interview, he was asked if his family was proud of him for making it into the NBA. He said, "My family is extremely proud. They know that they are responsible for me being here as much as I am." If Chris's family didn't push him to keep trying, he might have given up before making it into the NBA!

No matter how successful Chris gets, he will always remember everything his family has done for him, especially his grandfather. Chris talks about his grandfather on his website: "He was my best friend. I wouldn't be in the position I'm in now had it not been for him and the things he instilled in me—hard work and the importance of family." Chris has his own special way of remembering his grandfather. The national anthem is played before every NBA game. While the anthem plays, Chris says a prayer for all the family members he has lost, including Papa Chili.

HELPING THE WORLD

It is no secret that NBA players make a lot of money. Chris couldn't wait to start giving to charity after he signed his first NBA contract in 2005. He started the Chris Paul Foundation the same year. The foundation gives back to the community in a number of ways. One of the most well known is through the Nathaniel Jones Scholarship Fund. The scholarship is named after Chris's grandfather. It is given to students from Forsyth County who want to attend Wake Forest University, the same college Chris and Jada went to. Students who win the scholarship can follow in Chris's footsteps.

When disaster strikes, Chris is one of the first people to help. Chris joined the New Orleans Hornets just two months before Hurricane Katrina struck the team's home city. He saw firsthand how the hurricane destroyed homes and schools in the area. The Chris Paul Foundation started the CP3 AfterSchool Zone program to rebuild the city and give children from New Orleans the education they deserve. Another way Chris helps children is by encouraging them to be active and exercise. This is why he hosts the Annual CP3 Walk for Kids.

Chris coaches young basketball players at his basketball camp for poor kids in Los Angeles who love the game.

Chris loves bowling and has even raised money for charity through celebrity bowling tournaments.

Chris likes to find creative ways to use his *passions* to help others. For example, he loves bowling. He has said that if he wasn't a basketball player, he would be a professional bowler. Every year, he hosts a charity bowling tournament. Many stars come to bowl, including famous basketball and football players. Reggie Bush, Blake Griffin, and Michael Strahan have all come to bowl. The Chris Paul Foundation has also helped host a celebrity poker tournament.

Chris's future looks bright as one of the biggest stars in the NBA today. Chris knows what is important to him and focuses on doing his best on and off the court.

Chris isn't the only person in the Paul family who likes to help others. Jada has started a special event of her own. Every year, she gives several prom dresses to high school girls who cannot afford their own. During the event, the girls learn about the importance of staying healthy, eating right, getting a good education, and building self-esteem. They are given fashion tips as an added bonus.

CHRIS PAUL'S FUTURE

Chris Paul has learned to enjoy the attention he gets. Chris and his family have been guests on a few television shows, including *Family Feud*. In 2007 Chris even appeared on the cover of an NBA videogame. He is known as an unselfish player who is happy to do whatever it takes to win, whether it be passing the ball or taking a shot. Chris is a great example of a team player.

Athletes like Chris are paid to make a sport's brand look good. One famous sport company is Nike. The company makes shoes and clothing for athletes. Chris first signed a contract with Nike when he joined the NBA in 2005. Since then, he has helped design his own line of shoes, known as the Air Jordan CP3. Chris has had many endorsement deals during his career. He earns millions of dollars each year through his endorsement deals alone.

As of 2013, Chris does not plan to stop playing basketball anytime soon. He has been named an NBA All-Star a total of six times and even helped the United States bring home two Olympic gold medals. The one thing he hasn't done is earn a championship title. To do this, his home team would have to win the NBA finals. Chris Paul hopes to bring the Clippers to victory in the next few seasons.

Chris likes to help young athletes achieve their dreams. He has given speeches at sport camps and even written a book about how hard it was for him overcome the challenges of being short. According to Chris, the trick to making it in the basketball world is never giving up. Chris was once asked what advice he would give to someone who wanted to play in the NBA. He said, "Never let anyone tell you that you can't do something. Use it as **motivation** and stay focused." And Chris Paul is living proof it works!

Series Glossary of Key Terms

All-Star Game: A game where the best players in the league form two teams and play each other.

Assist: A pass that leads to scoring points. The player who passes the ball before the other scores a basket gets the assist.

Center: A player, normally the tallest on the team, who tries to score close to the basket and defend against the other team's offense using his size.

Championship: A set of games between the two top teams in the NBA to see who is the best.

Court: The wooden or concrete surface where basketball is played. In the NBA, courts are 94 feet by 50 feet.

Defensive: Working to keep the other team from scoring points.

Draft (noun): The way NBA teams pick players from college or high school teams.

Foul: A move against another player that is against the rules, mostly involving a player touching another in a way that is not fair play.

Jump shot: A shot made from far from the basket (rather than under the basket) while the player is in the air.

Offensive: Working to score points against the other team.

Playoffs: Games at the end of the NBA season between the top teams in the league, ending in the Finals, in which the two top teams play each other.

Point guard: The player leading the team's offense, scoring points and setting up other players to score.

Power forward: A player who can both get in close to the basket and shoot from further away. On defense, power forwards defend against both close and far shots.

Rebound: Getting the ball back after a missed shot.

Rookie: A player in his first year in the NBA.

Scouts: People who search for new basketball players in high school or college who might one day play in the NBA.

Shooting guard: A player whose job is to take shots from far away from the basket. The shooting guard is usually the team's best long-range shooter.

Small forwards: Players whose main job is to score points close to the basket, working with the other players on the team's offense.

Steal: Take the ball from a player on the other team.

Tournament: A series of games between different teams in which the winning teams move on to play other winning teams and losing teams drop out of the competition.

Find Out More

ONLINE

Chris Paul
chrispaul3.com

Chris Paul
twitter.com/cp3

Chris Paul Foundation
www.cp3foundation.org

Los Angeles Clippers
www.nba.com/clippers

NBA Hoop Troop
www.nbahooptroop.com

IN BOOKS

Herzog, Brad. *Hoopmania: The Book of Basketball History and Trivia*. New York: Rosen, 2003.

Ladewski, Paul. *Stars on the Court*. New York: Scholastic, 2009.

Paul, Chris, and Frank Morrison. *Long Shot: Never Too Small to Dream Big*. New York: Simon & Schuster for Young Readers, 2009.

Savage, Jeff. *Chris Paul*. Minneapolis, MN: Lerner Publications, 2010.

Schaller, Bob, and Dave Harnish. *The Everything Kids' Basketball Book: The All-Time Greats, Legendary Teams, Today's Superstars—and Tips on Playing like a Pro*. Avon, MA: Adams Media, 2009.

Index

About the Author

Aurelia Jackson is a writer living and working in New York City. She has a passion for writing and a love of education, both of which she brings to all the work she does.

Picture Credits